I0170757

For A Special Sales Minister:

From

Date

MAX J. LAMBDIN

A

GREATER

DETERMINATION

DEVOTIONAL READINGS FOR THE SALES PROFESSIONAL

HIS GREATNESS,
OUR DETERMINATION,
CHANGES LIVES

NEW CONSTANT
PUBLISHING

NEW CONSTANT
PUBLISHING

Published by New Constant Publishing, Perrysburg, Ohio 43551

DEDICATION

To my wife Deborah who saw this work completed
before it was created.

And our Lord Jesus Christ

CONTENTS

Acknowledgments
Foreword
Author's Preface
Author's Note
The Godly Succeed   1
What The Day Will Bring   3
Confident Hope   5
Hope in the Lord   7
Reward of Hope   9
A Clear Mind   11
Carry Out the Ministry   13
Everything Said   15
Sovereign Success   17
Like a Stone   19
Never Turn Aside   21
Not Ashamed   23
Take the Gifts   25
Power to Succeed   27
Strong Courage   29
Help Us   31
Divine Guidance   33
Work Willingly   35
Wise Words   37
No Words   39
Will Prosper   41
Urgent Needs   43
The Generous Producer   45
Bread to Eat   47
Harvest of Generosity   49
In Every Way   51
Plant a Seed   53
Reap a Harvest   55
An Entire Basket   57

A Peaceful Harvest   59
Run to Win   61
Purpose in Every Step   63
Amazing Works   65
Safety   67
Sweet as Honey   69
A Healthy Appetite   71
Keep Praying   73
Be Approved   75
The Good Worker   77
Word of Truth   79
Action   81
Diversified Activity   83
Wise Council   85
Trust in God   87
Humble Success   89
Impressive   91
Others First   93
All Others   95
The Greatest   97
Honestly   99
Strength in God   101
A Greater Determination   103
About the Author   106

ACKNOWLEDGMENTS

A Special Thanks

To David Bohman for editing skills and thoughtful considerations.

To Jim Lange and the Truth@Work group for their diligence, accountability and advice.

To Dirk Manning on the art of writing and crafting a book.

To my sales teammates for their feedback and encouragement during development.

And an additional special acknowledgement to Alia Wolaver. Without her persistence, skills, and encouragement, this work would not have been completed.

FOREWORD

For twenty years, I was a songwriter and lead singer for the band Sanctus Real. During that time, we sold almost a million albums, sold out concerts across the U.S. and sold music and merchandise to Christian music fans around the world.

You know as well as I do, that if you were to pull back the curtain on those statements, you'd find that *we,* as band members, didn't personally sell much of anything. Each of our successes, both big and small, were a gift from God; and most of them were a result of God-sent and gifted sales men and women, like you, building bridges between consumers and creators.

On every heart-touching story we've heard from someone impacted by our songs, are the fingerprints of a dedicated sales person. And because of their dedication, we were able to continue creating a product that we were passionate about.

As you read this book, written by my friend Max, my prayer is that you feel affirmed in your calling, and continue to grow in the gifts that God has given you with good purpose in this world. May you be blessed and challenged by the words found in these pages.

-   Matt Hammitt
Grammy Nominated, Dove Award winning vocalist, founding member of Sanctus Real, author, speaker, and host and producer of "The Lead Me Lifecast".

AUTHOR'S PREFACE

"That's because sales people are..."

I have been in service sales and been leading sales teams for over a decade. In that time, I have experienced the thrill of success and witnessed frustration from sales as a profession and career.

For too much of that time, I failed to see sales as a calling and only perceived it as a necessary obligation. I consistently created an idol out of what I deemed to be truer ministry inside of the church.

Those years were beneficial in creating a well-rounded perception and developing experience. However, my God, family, church family, friends and business would have been better served had I recognized sales for what it is: a ministry.

The importance of accepting this ministry call and writing this devotional came one autumn Monday morning before a sales-team meeting. I have had the benefit to work for organizations that allow me to share inspirational devotional thoughts during my meetings. I had been searching for fresh devotionals for weeks before that were targeted directly to sales people. I looked online and in bookstores. Nothing. I found a few about business and faith, but not sales.

Before that meeting I asked one of my friends and colleagues at the time, "Why do you think there is so little to encourage Christians in sales?" His response was beyond telling and set me back for the rest of the day. "That's because Christians think sales people are evil, and ministers don't want to encourage them."

Wow. Just like that a Christian in sales is not only less than ministry, but evil. Less than noble. He didn't mean to be self-loathing about his career. He just was speaking the perceived reality for many in this ministry.

Maybe his words were strong. But the gap from evil to ministry presents a pretty significant mental and spiritual leap.

Granted, there is a lot of corruption and greed in sales organizations. A good number of people enter the industry to indulge in explicit lifestyles, manipulation and avarice.

But of course there is a better way. Sales cannot be exclusive for the use of evil. Not with so many amazing faithful believers in Christ giving life to others through their work. Not with so many servants like us providing a good word to those we reach. No, the truth is, those of us who temporarily or permanently serve God in sales, are providing ministry to our communities. Sure, others may attempt to sully our name, but not us. We serve the Lord.

The word for service and ministry are one and the same. We sales professionals provide services to meet the needs, desires and wants of individuals and organizations around the globe. From those selling tires to keep cars safely on the road, to financial advisors caring for stewardship to medical offices caring for bodies. We sales ministers serve God in our daily lives.

We are Sales Ministers and we are valuable to both God and man. Without us, the world does not revolve, businesses do not profit and churches do not receive gifts.

May you be encouraged by the thoughts in these pages. And may they contribute to growth in your Sales Ministry.

-   Max J. Lambdin

AUTHOR'S NOTE

A Greater Determination includes devotional exhortations, relevant Bible verses and meditations. Each devotional is set in two-page pairs.

The meditations following the Scriptural text can be read as thoughts, psalms or prayers. However, please feel free to pray in your own way or pray your own prayer.

These devotions are intentionally brief to facilitate the results-oriented life of the sales professional. Read this daily, weekly or however you like, but please be encouraged in your walk and sales practice by each of these pages.

The Godly Succeed

❦❧

THE FIRST GOAL in our sales ministry is to be Godly. We can put on Jesus daily and walk in His Spirit before all else.

He will provide.

In His provision there is no shame in our success. We succeed in helping others fulfill needs. That is a ministry of The Lord.

All who are around us, will find themselves rejoicing in the accomplishment. After all, this accomplishment comes because we serve our clients, our companies, our households and The Lord.

When the godly succeed, everyone is glad. — *Proverbs 28:12*

∽⟩⟨∾

Lord, I pray today to find Godliness that only I can find in You. You are the source of all my hopes, dreams and desires.

I know that You alone that can cause me to find success. I pray my success is a joy and benefit to others.

May You be blessed by all I do this day in my business and in my life.

I pray for Your provision and success this day.

What the Day Will Bring

❦

WE DON'T KNOW. This wisdom is priceless for all walks of life. For the sales professional it is essential.

Working today for its own provision is a freedom from worry. We really count on something we do not yet have for the future.

Also, resting on the success of today will not benefit our production tomorrow. Just as we can ignore the failures of yesterday, for yesterday is now gone.

The Lord will provide all our needs.

Don't brag about tomorrow, since you don't know what the day will bring. —*Proverbs 27:1*

જીજી

Lord, I pray You become the provision for all my needs.

I know that You possess everything I could ever desire. Please remove the worry and doubt about what the day will bring.

Lord I pray, You bolster my spirit to take on the challenges of the day. And I pray that I not rest on what I have done, so that I may be diligent tomorrow.

Confident Hope

⤜⤛

So MUCH OF who we are seems tied to what we do and how much we accomplish. We focus the majority of time ranking our worth by production.

We do this knowing those results are temporary.

But we serve The One who is eternal. When we know this truth, no other affirmations matter. No other words can mean as much.

We can walk in the confidence of our ranking with The Lord, and His accomplishments.

He is our Confident Hope.

Rejoice in our confident hope. —*Romans 12:12*

$$\iff$$

Lord, You are the hope for all of my life, my business, my clients, my family.

No matter the success I have, my hope is in You.

No matter the obstacles I face, my hope is in You.

No matter where man has me ranked, high or low, my hope is in You.

You are my confident hope!

Hope in the Lord

๛๛

WE CAN FEEL hopefulness from so many things. A sunny day, a new job, and of course a closed deal will all lift our spirits.

But those are mere fleeting satisfactions. No emotional experience is unimportant, but none compare to the foundation of Hope, which is Jesus Christ.

One of the most amazing and powerful abilities we have from The Lord is Hope. With it, not only can we sustain, but we can achieve dreams we haven't even had yet.

And so, Lord, where do I put my hope? My only hope is in you. — *Psalm 39:7*

❧❧

Lord, I pray today for You to be my only hope.

I find hope when circumstances change. I find hope when I get new opportunities. I find hope when something is new.

But all of those things change.

Lord, I place my hope in You, and not just mere experiences.

Reward of Hope

∽∂∂∽

THERE ARE MANY rewards and joys in our Sales Ministry!

Many days we help to close the gap on a special need for our new or existing client. Only we are able to help another person in that way! Only we took the risk to help them identify that need. And only we were able to move them to a life-changing and positive decision.

But with all of that being true, our reward from God is His Hope. And that reward sustains more than any incentive or single experience.

His promise will not falter in our life and our days will be filled with that reward.

You will be rewarded for this; your hope will not be disappointed. — *Proverbs 23:18*

⤜⤛

So many circumstances disappoint me. I can easily find myself disillusioned.

When I place my hope in temporary results, I easily get discouraged.

But today, I place my hope in You Lord. And I know, that hope will not be disappointed.

You are forever my hope and You are forever my reward.

A Clear Mind

❦❦

PRESSURE, STRESS, TRAUMA dry seasons and even times of success can cloud our vision and perception.

Others emotions and actions can cause us to react. Perhaps a friend, parent, spouse or client misrepresents our intentions. Maybe a sale fell through. This can be frustrating and cause a negative response.

Remember God has called us. We are friends and servants of The Lord!
We are friends and servants to others in their specific need.

The humility of servant hood helps us to stay clear in mind and steer clear of obstacles to our fruitfulness.

Keep a clear mind in every situation. — *2 Timothy 4:5*

∽⟩⟨∼

Lord, You are perfect in mind and spirit. Make me as You are. So much of what I face today affects how I respond to You and others.

I desire Your will for my life. I pray that regardless of the circumstance that I put on the mind of Christ.

I pray to be as You are in every situation.

Carry Out The Ministry

❧

OUR CURRENT CALL and ministry is the sales profession. It is both a powerful call and often a challenging ministry.

Our call is not only to produce in our service, but it is also to share Christ in every way.

We can share the Good News of Christ in word and action while presenting our service for our organizations and our clients.

As we see and function in both parts of life together, the more we will "fully carry out the ministry".

Work at telling others the Good News, and fully carry out the ministry God has given you. — *2 Timothy 4:5*

୶ঌ৵

You Lord, are the Minister. Anything I would call my ministry without You is meaningless. As You work through me and for me in the marketplace, I become a minister.

As I serve others Lord, work through me.

As I steward my organization Lord, work through me.

As I live Lord, minister through me.

In Your efforts Lord, may I carry out Your ministry in this call as a sales person and as Your servant.

Everything Said

∽⧫⧫

EVERYTHING! That is a simple, all-encompassing word that means, well, everything.

And our powerful words can be used to build or destroy. An encouragement or a discouragement. To help or hinder. For profit or for loss. For success or failure.

The wisdom of scripture does not only extend to our clients, but to anyone who hears our words.

Take these moments to reflect on what is being heard in everything said.

Let everything you say be good and helpful, so that your words will be an encouragement to those who hear them. — *Ephesians 4:29*

❧ ❧

Lord, Your words are like a fountain. Living water that passes from Your heart to my ears and into my soul.

Kingdom Father I pray today that my words will be life-giving to all those I encounter in my practice.

May my language reflect Your mind, and may I do more than close a deal today. May I change a life.

Sovereign Success

∽❦❧

"WILL I FAIL?" is a vicious and reoccurring struggle for many, if not all, sales professionals.

"Will I be ashamed?" is a sibling to the first doubt, with similar sinister entrapments.

"Will they say, 'I told us so!'?" is the child of the other two and is filled with envy and fear.

But, if we hold to the truth of our Lord's faithfulness, then we do not need to succumb to fear. Shame and failure never come from believing the words of God over doubts spoken by men.

Some form of victory always comes from the promises of Jesus. So we can let Him tell us so.

Because the Sovereign Lord helps me, I will not be disgraced.. — *Isaiah 50:7*

కోత

Lord, I am pursuing success in an occupation others have feared.

In their fear many have failed.

By my faith in You, I know that You have placed me in this call.

I believe that You have set me in this ministry.

And by my faith in You Sovereign King, I will succeed. In You I will never be disgraced.

Like a Stone

THIS DAY, THIS WEEK may our determination to follow the will of God overcome every doubt, every challenge and every obstacle.

Our business may be up or down. Our sale may have closed or was postponed, but He is The Rock for us.

When we set our will firmly upon His promises, we are like an immovable stone.

Minds and hearts firmly set towards The Lord are placed deeply in the ground of His foundations.

Therefore, I have set my face like a stone, determined to do His will. — *Isaiah 50:7*

∽◌◌

Lord, every time I go to make a call or meet a new prospect, I am intimidated. When yesterday or the past week was rough on my business, I am even more hesitant.

But in You, I have set my self like a rock against adversity.

Where others are cautious, I will be bold and execute the plans You have given me!

Never Turn Aside

❧❧

IN OUR BUSINESS we can be easily distracted and torn in many directions.

But like four living creatures in Ezekiel's vision, God has made us perfectly for His purposes.

Even when that purpose isn't clear, we know He has His specific vision for us.

In our Sales Ministry, we must:

Face the direction set for us.
Move in that direction without pause.
and
Stay focused on that purpose in faith.

They went straight in the direction they faced, never turning aside. — *Ezekiel 10:11*

⊰∽⊱

So many distractions want my attention from You and Your purpose Lord.

I often feel like I have four different faces trying to go in many directions.

Lord, please set me on the path You have for me.

I have faith in You, that even when I can't see clearly, that the path will lead me to Your purpose.

Not Ashamed

❧❧

A SALES MINISTRY is a noble service and profession. And in it, may we have the gift of freedom from the opinions and biases of others.

Of course, there have been unethical professionals in the past. And many voices in our lives would like us to believe that's the only way. But not us, we serve nobly pleasing The Lord.

Remember, we meet the needs of others through solutions, services and products.

There is no shame about any of those accomplishments.

And I know that I will not be put to shame. — *Isaiah 50:7*

∽⁀∾

Lord, so many express the thoughts of sales as manipulation or control.

Jesus, I pray, that I would be articulate with Your words and works to serve others.

May it never be said of me that I have done anything other than serve You and Your people faithfully in my practice and ministry to them.

Take the Gifts

∽৬ট৯

SALES PROFESSIONALS often feel hesitant to start a conversation or introduce their product.

But know this, our Sales Ministry is a gift to those we are called to serve.

Our products and services are purposed by God to provide for the needs of others.

Our talents are a gift from God, and in that we must share our knowledge with others.

As we take good news to our clients and help them, they will thank God and know Him even more.

And when we take your gifts to those who need them, they will thank God. — *2 Corinthians 9:11*

ॐॐ

Lord, sometimes I don't feel like I have much to offer.

But I know that You are in me and work through me.

Please provide me the right way to say the right thing to the right person today.

In those words I will provide for my clients, my family and my church.

Bless You Lord and all the gifts You give Your people.

Power to Succeed

POWER! That word itself has impact.

It is the force that drives behavior, solutions, results and moves people and business to action.

Power is a must for any sales profession.

But our power in Christ does not result in controlling, dominating or manipulating those around us. Our power does not put others below us.

He gives us the power of His sacrifice in death burial and resurrection. Our power is to serve, give and deliver.

Jesus is the source, and in every meeting, we simply deliver His gifts.

He is the one who gives you power to be successful. — *Deuteronomy 8:18*

ಌಛ

Lord, I often struggle for control over my life, my sales, and my career. But today, I surrender that power to You.

I don't want power over others. Unless it is the power to forgive, to show grace or to give away the knowledge I have of You.

Today, I know You will show me power to live in a way I have not before.

Today it is You who gives me the power to succeed.

Strong Courage

❦

STRONG COURAGEOUS FAITH causes us respond to our call in this field.

Strong courageous faith helps us resist temptation to give up, when giving up seems like the only way.

Strong courageous faith enables us to believe, when others do not.

Strong courageous faith overcomes every doubt, even when doubt seems louder than conviction.

Strong courageous faith emboldens us when others question why we do this everyday.

Let strong courageous faith in the Lord carry our hearts today.

Stand firm in the faith. Be courageous. Be strong. — *1 Corinthians 16:13*

✧✧

Lord thank You for making me strong in my weakness. In myself I know no courage.

But in You Lord, I am able to overcome any attack against my mind or circumstance.

In You Lord, I can accomplish tasks and attain success I never knew to be possible.

I love You Lord, thank You for the provision of faith.

Help Us

∽⟨⟩∾

SO MANY DAYS begin with what do "I" need. But in Scripture, the prophet says "our" need.

We are messengers of The Lord, regardless of the product or service we sell.

There are needs we have and there are needs our clients have. And both have a need for the Lord's help as in the past.

Today and this week, we are the persons to bring The Lord to a client and meet their need.

In that sowing that seed, our needs will also be met with a great harvest.

In this time of our deep need, help us again as you did in years gone by — *Habakkuk 3:2*

There are some days I feel my needs so very deeply. Lord, how can You provide for needs that are so significant?

I know only You can!

There are days I can't even begin to think I can help any one else. Lord, how can You work through me?

I know only You can!

There are times, I need You in ways I have needed You before. Lord how can You help me again?

I know only You can!

Divine Guidance

∽⌇⌇∾

THERE ARE MANY schemes and products in the marketplace. Developing our skills with God's guidance is more important than any other focus of our Sales Ministry.

Can we take the time today, to stop reading the flyers, emails and answering the calls about the latest strategy?

Let us pray for even just a moment in quiet to accept guidance from the One who knows perfectly His direction for our ministry.

And in doing so, may we take His peace into whatever appointments we have this week.

When people do not accept divine guidance, they run wild. — *Proverbs 29:18*

∽⌒∂

Lord, may Your ways be known to me, as my knowledge and ways merely lead me into wandering.

Lord equip me and be my guide.

My words are meaningless. But Your words are life.

Please teach me daily to follow You and to seek Your kingdom before all else, so that my life will follow Your order and Your ways.

Work Willingly

❧❧

WE HAVE THE SKILLS and gifts from God to achieve the goals He has set for us. If we have not yet developed those skills, others around us can help.

But it is our sole responsibility to be willing to work out our call completely. Skills can be taught and gifts can be developed. Also circumstances, people and their motivations all will change.

But The Lord does not change and He does have us in this Sales Ministry. Our willingness to do or not do completely determines our ability to succeed.

Work willingly at whatever you do, as though you were working for the Lord rather than for people. — *Colossians 3:23*

જાજી

Lord, I know Your ways are unchanging. Your heart for me is firm.

Form in me the ability to always see You and Your ways in all the work I put my hands to.

Sometimes, I cannot see You in the client I serve, but I pray that I will.

I am willing, and so I seek You first for all my business and my life.

Wise Words

∽ℰ∾

THE RIGHT WORDS. Seems so easy, until we don't have them.

The Lord in His time on earth spent many hours seeking the Father for the right words. So too, we must take time to pray. He always will give us our provision of wisdom.

Likewise, The Lord has also given others great wisdom in their Sales Ministry. We can follow the example of those around us who are skilled at closing the gap for their client's problems.

If we don't have our own, we can use their right words, help a family with our service and win a meal for today.

Wise words will win you a good meal. — *Proverbs* *13:2*

∽⁊⁊∾

Lord, Your model prayer teaches to ask "give us this day our daily bread".

Today Lord, I ask that You give the opportunity to serve. To close a gap on a need. That I may win a good meal for my household. That I might win a good meal for those in another household.

Use me Lord in this ministry to serve You and Your people with wisdom.

No Words

WHEN OUR CLIENT is ready to accept our recommendation, follow this proverb, say "yes and thank you". Then its time to close our mouths.

These families that we help service will be more impressed by our self-control and resolve than by further indulgent demonstrations of product knowledge.

Knowing when not to speak is equal to knowing what to say.

In those moments of quiet, Our Lord may just fill the next sentences with His words for that client.

Opening your mouth can ruin everything. — *Proverbs 13:3*

❧❧

Lord, I love to talk. It's one of the reasons You called me to this Sales Ministry.

Please teach me Your wise ways, to know when I have said enough. When my words are satisfactory for the moment.

Lord, I only want to serve and help these families. May my words never get in the way.

Will Prosper

❧❧

THE TRUTH IS ETERNAL. When we are a good steward of the work The Lord has given us we prosper in Him.

When we do so in diligence, we will succeed.

The sales profession as a call can be one of the hardest jobs in the world. We may even be letting it get us down today.

But our Sales Ministry, is our service and our call.

As we walk out that call in obedience today, many will prosper.

Those who work hard will prosper. — *Proverbs 13:4*

❧❧

There are days I want to lay flat on my back and ask "why?" rather than do. Lord, when these days come, I pray You lift me up and place me on my feet.

May my wants match Your desires for my life today. I want to work hard, but only if it is the work You have for me.

Being in You alone, will be my prosperity.

Urgent Needs

WE MEET NEEEDS! The essence and definition of a Sales Ministry is meeting the recognizable needs of others.

And there are so many ways we can meet the needs of others. We can serve our church, teach children, we can serve in missions. Sometimes just being hospitable meets many needs.

The passage from Paul to Titus on the next page may be the most prescriptive and definitive verse for a Sales Minister.

When we meet needs with our service and product, we fulfill our calling today and become fruitful.

Our people must learn to do good by meeting the urgent needs of others; then they will not be unproductive. — *Titus 3:14*

❧❧

Lord, I want to be a productive part of Your Kingdom.

Please instill in me today the way and paths to meet the needs of others.

Show me how and why they need what they need.

Sometimes, I think what I do is small or insignificant, but I pray You show me how it affects the lives of all those I touch.

The Generous Producer

AS THE LORD has cheerfully given to us, so we must also gladly take our talents and give.

Success in Sales Ministry will provide for our needs as we provide for the needs of others.

As we are enterprising with our gifts, and respectful of the call, God provides for every need.

But our purpose is even greater. The promise and abundance of the Gospel is one of giving.

His promise, is that as we give, He will give us more...and we will give more.

What an amazing life!

And God will generously provide all you need. Then you will always have everything you need and plenty left over to share with others. — *2 Corinthians 9:8*

❧❧

Lord, I can't see clearly how what I do each day will provide generously. Often I feel like I take more than I can give.

But, You have more to give than can be seen in my world.

I pray that the promise to have plenty left will swiftly be manifest in my life.

Lord help me to see the plenty I have today, so that I might give it away.

You are an amazing Lord! Thank You for an amazing life!

Bread to Eat

❧

AT THE BEGINNING of each sales cycle we plant. And at the end we will reap a harvest.

This principle is not just some ideology manufactured by the business world. It is actually a universal and irrefutable process put in to work by God to provide for His people.

As a Sales Minister, we don't need seasons to plant and harvest. We can always plant and always eat.

We can always help and always meet a need.

Just as God always provides our seed.

For God is the one who provides seed for the farmer and then bread to eat. — *2 Corinthians 9:10*

∽ ∾

Lord, You are the Bread of Life. As I eat of You, I thrive in everlasting ways.

I am reminded to come to You for provision first before I try and make my own bread.

Thank You for creating seed and harvest.

Thank You for Your seeds to plant.

Thank You for placing me in a call where I can always meet a need. Please bring a new person with a new need to me today.

Harvest of Generosity

❦

EVERYTHING WE ARE and do comes from the work of Christ in us.

He provides our gifts, and causes them to grow.

Each success we have, each case we close and each person we help with a sale comes from His resources in us.

His increase causes growth we can't imagine. When he orchestrates a thing, nothing we do can compare.

It is His harvest we need. Anything we do on our own falls steeply short. But he gives so we give away.

All He does...is to fulfill the generous life in us.

He will provide and increase your resources and then produce a great harvest of generosity in you.
— *2 Corinthians 9:10*

᨞

Lord, oh how powerfully You give. I may water the land with Your words, and speak of Your ways, but only You can add the increase.

Lord, I must have more of You. I can give, but only You can truly fill me.

Please teach me how You give.

I know that You gave Your life. Please continue to produce generosity in me.

In Every Way

❧❧

LIKE A GOOD FARMER Jesus enriches the soil of our lives.

He does this so completely that we can continuously be productive in our lives and business.

And like the production of a healthy garden, our increase is never meant for personal profit.

Our growth is always for the purpose of providing for others, feeding others, and providing seed for the next harvest.

Just as He has enriched us in every way, so may we enrich others.

Yes, you will be enriched in every way so that you can always be generous. — *2 Corinthians 9:11*

∽৹৫৹

Like soil that is turned and replanted, You have enriched my fields.

Thank You for the power to be generous with words, talents, actions, service and finances.

Thank You for gifts to give away.

Thank You for an occupation that provides the opportunity to serve others everyday.

Lord, may I be excellent at enriching others in every way.

Plant a Seed

JUST LIKE EVERYDAY has a morning, so does our business.

If we plant the right diverse seeds in our "morning", we will be productive in the "afternoon".

If we only spend time on production and no time on planting we will have no harvest in the "afternoon".

We must spend some time in prayer and ask The Lord what seeds we should be planting this "morning" to "keep busy all afternoon".

Plant your seed in the morning and keep busy all afternoon...— *Ecclesiastes 11:6*

Lord, I can keep busy with the best of them. I ask that You would show me the seeds I should plant to be occupied with Your call.

My mornings and afternoons may be days or years.

I pray that You give me the seed that will bring forth Your harvest for the rightly timed afternoon.

In that, I will be busy with Your purpose and produce what You desire.

Reap a Harvest

❧❧

MANY CIRCUMSTANCES, situations, thoughts and feelings will keep us from doing what we need to daily.

Our business and life are never going to line up to be perfect in every way.

Act Now, not when circumstances are perfect.

Decide now, not just when it feels right.

Be now, the best professional and person of God.

And even in a storm, we will reap a harvest.

Farmers who wait for perfect weather never plant. If they watch every cloud, they never harvest. — *Ecclesiastes 11:4*

⫷⫸

Lord, sometimes the storm seems bigger than You. As when Peter walked on the water and saw the wind and the waves, rather than Your face.

Lord, teach me and prepare me to plant a productive seed even when there are storms all around me.

Lord, forgive me for not taking opportunity when I should have in the past, and I choose to take opportunity, regardless of challenge, that You place in front of me in the future.

An Entire Basket

IT IS AMAZING when The Lord makes a way for our production.

So many days we drive, struggle and push. We want to see something happen, and there doesn't seem to be any profit.

But then comes a day that The Lord orchestrates and nothing stops us from gathering a harvest.

On that day, our needs are met and the blessings make up for the past.

All days are working together for a great harvest from The Lord. Stand strong in every hour, for that day comes.

... and when she beat out the grain that evening, it filled an entire basket. — *Ruth 2:17*

❧❧

Lord, when You orchestrate a thing, my baskets are full.

Show me the fields to reap Your grain.

I pray I can choose with wisdom the right calls to make, the right people to speak with and the right things to say.

Your harvest is greater. Thank You for the bounty You have given me.

Lord, I pray You do so again.

A Peaceful Harvest

❧❧

DISCIPLINE IS AN absolute necessity in our Sales Ministry as it is in all facets of life.

But we need to allow God to discipline and hold to his direction and execute on his instruction.

We can be the person, do the things and live the call others refuse. Let others reject an ongoing peaceful harvest.

Performing unpopular disciplined tasks manifests character that is unique, powerful and far too uncommon. The alternative is failure, which is the harshest discipline of all.

Our goals may be difficult to accomplish this week, but the reward is great.

No discipline is enjoyable while it is happening—it's painful! But afterward there will be a peaceful harvest...— *Hebrews 12:11*

Lord, I don't always like it when You discipline me, but I have to have Your words of correction.

I don't always fulfill Your purpose daily, but when I am disciplined by You to perform Your works, I am fulfilled.

Work in me and through me to be more like You in transformation daily.

I know Your ways will not only produce a provision, but will multiply a peaceful harvest.

Run to Win

❦

PAUL EXHORTS US not just to run for recreation, but to gain the goal.

Our purpose as a Sales Minister is a noble profession that helps individuals meet daily needs. This is not just another job. We are not just running to see the road. He has us here for a reason.

As we pursue each day, it is good to set goals and commitments. As we accomplish them we win.

When we open and close a sale, and do it righteously, we create a winning situation for our client, and our family.

Also, it is good stewardship of the call God has on us today. And that, in itself, is a huge win!

So run to win! — *1 Corinthians 9:24*

సౌ<0ు>

Lord, thank You for creating me with a purpose and a goal.

I appreciate that You have given me a finish line everyday and in my life. Otherwise I would be running aimlessly without direction.

I praise You that every time I run, I can finish in You.

And Lord, may I not just finish, but may I finish well.

Purpose in Every Step

∽⌒∾

NOT EVERY ACTION we take in our Sales Ministry seems to produce results.

That's because not every action serves that purpose. Some actions are frivolous.

We need to take the time to identify steps to stay in focus for God's goals and will.

When those are clear, we not only walk out our purpose, but run each step faster than we have previously imagined.

So I run with purpose in every step. — *1 Corinthians 9:26*

✌❧

Lord, create in me the ability to run fervently toward Your purpose.

I don't want to simply be in sales or go on calls.

Show me Your goals. Show me who to help, and how to help them.

Lord, let me have my identity in purpose in You.

And may I produce the results in my actions that You desire.

Amazing Works

OUR CUSTOMERS have heard "all about us" and they can see "all about us". It's called our reputation and becomes our brand.

Does our integrity meet with what we have heard about The Lord?

We all have a past, but it is time to lay it down. We no longer need to carry yesterday's successes or failure.
Today, we pray for the integrity, character and peace of Jesus Christ to resonate in us and our work.

After all, we are really working in, through and for Him.

In this truth, our clients will accept "all about us" as "all about The Lord".

I have heard all about you, Lord. I am filled with awe by your amazing works. — *Habakkuk 3:2*

∽⌒∾

Lord, I am truly amazed by You.

In every way You do things and what I have seen of You. I realized that the closer I get to You, the more I see wrong with myself.

I don't know how others can see You in me, but I pray they do.

I pray that as I work for others today, that You would touch them through my words and hands.

Safety

WE ARE CALLED to a Sales Ministry and we hear many messages. Some are the encouraging words of a trusting Lord.

But others come from well-intentioned people speaking negative and ungodly thoughts about success.

Our own fears of the unknown and rejection can cloud our vision for this calling everyday.

But we can trust in our King's safety and we can be diligent to execute according to His promise.

That is the only message we need.

Fearing people is a dangerous trap, but trusting the Lord means safety. — *Proverbs 29:25*

∽৯৹৴৵

Lord, the words of other people affect me everyday, because I want to please them.

Father, give me grace today to hear Your message about this call today. May Your voice be louder than any other.

May Your influence broadcast into my heart in ways that I have not experienced before.

I do not know what is coming next, but may my message to all others be Your words of safety and courage.

Sweet as Honey

A GREAT HURDLE in our Sales Ministry is the loss of urgency from complacency.

When we are full of our own success the sweetest things often pass us by. This happens because we no longer feel an immediate need.

It is a mistake to find satisfaction in our past achievements, no matter how great, no matter how recent.

The most fulfilling rewards in our business come from a God-given hunger and this desire must never be quenched.

The next accomplishment may just be honey from The Lord.

A person who is full refuses honey... — *Proverbs 27:7*

Lord, You have given me so much. I often cannot believe the extent of Your provision for my family.

But, Lord instill in me Your divine hunger and desire for what is next in my purpose and Your will.

I do not want to be so satisfied that I miss Your next move and Your next opportunity for provision. I don't want to miss Your opportunity to serve.

Your word is sweet as honey in my soul.

A Healthy Appetite

IN OUR SALES MINISTRY it is so tempting to rest upon our past performance.

Top producers and leaders all know that the holding to the past will only result in a false security. But the emptiness of an unknown future can be filled by pursuing the next relationship God has for us.

It is not only necessary to follow that appetite, it is good and virtuous to embrace the hunger.

Without an emptiness, there is no opportunity for God to fill the space.

It is good for workers to have an appetite; an empty stomach drives them on. — *Proverbs 16:26*

⤋⤉

Faith in You is easy to come by Lord. You provide it so readily.

But somehow the unknown still causes me to become stir crazy.

Nonetheless, today I thank You Lord for the vacuum of a mysterious future. While I do not know what the future holds, I know that because it is there, You can fill it with Your promises and goals for me.

Thank You for the opportunity to have faith in You! I do believe!

Keep Praying

KEEP ON PRAYING.

Yes, all times are times to pray. Perhaps we have no new business, or a sale just fell through.

Keep on Praying.

When we have more sales than we imagined.

Keep on Praying.

When we have abundance.

Keep on Praying.

When we are in a slump.

Keep on Praying.

...and keep on praying. — *Romans 12:12*

❧❧

Your word teaches me to pray without ceasing.

This Sales Ministry is in Your hands. My life is in Your hands.

Lord, teach me to pray.

Be Approved

 divider

WORK HARD. These words can mean many things. Hours, tasks, and thoughts.

But the hardest work to receive approval from God is not performance.

Our results stem from the hard work of doing what we must because it is right, because we are called to this ministry at this moment.

Right now there is one thing we do not want to do, but we must to serve our business, clients and others.

Doing that thing, in word or deed...that thing is the "work hard" moment. Present it to God and in that we will be approved.

Work hard so you can present yourself to God and receive his approval...— *2 Timothy 2:15*

❦

Lord, I know You love me no matter what. You are unconditional with Your affection in ways I cannot understand.

But I ask Lord, that I may be equipped to serve in my Sales Ministry in a pleasing way to You.

I pray that I might bring to You all my talents, skills and appointments to You as an offering that is pleasing.

Lord, bring favor in life, business, and to all those I meet today.

The Good Worker

ৡৣৡ

CIRCUMSTANCES in our sales practice may be going poorly or things may be going well.

Either condition is merely a result of our effectiveness on the job. Both are temporary. Neither point to how good we actually are as people.

A good Sales Ministry worker sells something they believe in, that they buy themselves and that does not violate their integrity.

Results fluctuate, but we can always be a good worker. Do well in that thing and the results will follow.

Be a good worker... — *2 Timothy 2:15*

You are The Good Worker.

Lord, please work through me.

All my efforts are meaningless without You.

Lord, please work through me.

My days are all fruitless without You.

Lord, please work through me.

My reward is only You.

Lord, please work through me.

Word of Truth

MANY SALES PROFESSIONALS have lost credibility, reputation and profitability because of dishonesty for short-term gain.

But the diligent servant of the sale explains the truth.

In all things, we must speak as if we are sharing the good things of the Gospel.

This is true regardless if it is our presentation for our service or product, or it is our proclamation of our faith.

After all, our business practice is merely an extension of our belief in the One who provided the call for our profession.

One who...correctly explains the word of truth. — *2 Timothy 2:15*

❦

Your word is truth. Truly, I'm not worthy to explain it to any one. How can I when I rarely understand it. How can I when it changes for me in amazing ways.

Lord, I don't know how what I would say on a sales call could be Your word.

But if You will it, use me to speak the truth and share Your word with all I meet.

Action

◈◈

ONE KEY to wisdom is the word "action". We do not need to only commit our desires, wishes, ambitions, motivations or worries.

Our plans without action will remain ideas. Many times we intend to make another sales call, have another conversation, or seek out another lead. But without action, those plans may as well be dust clouds.

Our actions, implemented with the right distinction and sanctification, will bring us success.

When we move in alignment with His plans, we cannot, we will not fail.

Commit your actions to the Lord, and your plans will succeed. — *Proverbs 16:3*

⚭⚮

Lord, I have the same hesitance as many others in my business.

Sometimes, I just don't want to do the things I must.

Lord, raise me up, guide me and lead me to act now. So that the plans You have for me will not be left and unaccomplished.

I pray to be a good steward of the activity You have for me today.

Diversified Activity

∽⃝∾

AN EASY MISSTEP is to believe that our results come from one or two things that we are doing in service.

Today those successes come from one vital activity, but tomorrow we may need to leverage another.

As we walk out this call in grace, we have to keep in mind that our profit comes from cause and effect.

It comes from doing many things and doing them well week in and week out.

Let us pray on this practical Biblical wisdom and grow in strength in our business.

You don't know if profit will come from one activity or another—or maybe both. — *Ecclesiastes 11:6*

❧❧

Lord I need wisdom!

Teach me and show me what plow to put my hand to today.

I need Your guidance to lead me in the ways that will provide profit for my clients, my family and this ministry.

Thank You, Lord, that there is so much opportunity and avenues to serve.

May I choose the right one today.

Wise Council

✖✖

SALES PROFESSIONALS often accomplish amazing feats. There really is nothing like bringing, landing and closing a case. Providing solutions for a family or business can be one of the most satisfying feelings a producer can experience.

However, we also can be quite self-satisfied about how we accomplished our success. When in fact, these gifts to sell are granted by our Creator. And our skills were imparted by some teacher or mentor.

No matter what the tenure of our career, it is always good to seek Godly advice or counsel and never stop learning. In that humility to learn from others is our greatest accomplishment.

There is safety in having many advisers. — *Proverbs 11:14*

❧☙

Thank You Lord for placing so many great experienced sales people in my life.

I appreciate Your words of wisdom and practice that I receive through those mentors.

Lord, today I ask that You help me to identify who I should listen to more.

And please send me more leaders to learn even greater practices to serve You and my clients.

Trust in God

❧❧

WORRY, FRETTING, and negative concerns all come with being in a sales profession.

No career is more frustrating than sales, but in those moments, trust in God.

We can do all the right things without the results. Trust in God.

We may not know where the next prospect is coming from. Trust in God.

We may have lost a deal. Trust in God.

We may want to quit today. Trust in God.

We are called to this service. Trust in God.

Don't let your hearts be troubled. Trust in God.
— *John 14:1*

❧❧

Lord, I trust You.

I do not know why things are the way they are.

I trust You.

I do not know what tomorrow may bring.

I trust You.

Lord, teach me what it means to be anxious for nothing.

I trust You.

Humble Success

❧

SUCCESS LENDS ITSELF to pride rather than humility. However, as a Sales Minister, remembering how we came to success will always help us keep perspective.

After all, it is The Lord and His other servants that have spoken in to our lives that helped us arrive where we are today.

The failures of the past are gone and serve to magnify the joy of future accomplishments. In the same way, the successes of the past are merely stepping stones to help us conquer the challenges of the future.

It is good to place clients, colleagues and God before ourselves. In this is our greatest accomplishment.

Be humble, thinking of others as better than yourselves. — *Philippians 2:3*

❧❧

Lord, I desire amazing things for all those who are around me.

But so many days, I consider myself and my needs before Your people.

Lord, teach me today to be like You in this way. That I might seek my brothers' needs before my own.

And in meeting those needs I will serve and love You more.

Impressive

❧❧

COMPARISONS ARE an easy trap for sales professionals. In that service we demonstrate confidence and competence concerning our products and services.

But it is a snare to try and prove we are better than those around us.

Our ability to listen. Our heart of concern. And our willingness to serve and help clients make a much greater impression than listing all of our accomplishments or demonstrating the robustness of our knowledge.

And believe this, we are already impressive, because we are children of God.

Don't try to impress others. — *Philippians 2:3*

~§~

Lord, I confess, I want others to like me. After all, I am likeable, and that benefits this call.

But Lord, I ask that I base my worth on how You see me. And on How You care for me.

I don't want to be concerned whether others esteem me in certain ways. I will seek to do well in all things, but as long as I have Your favor I am whole.

Others First

❦

IN OUR SALES MINISTRY, we take a lot of action through transactions. In essences, all sales are a transaction between two cooperative parties.

However, it is the utmost importance to always have the customer's best interest in mind. It is an easy fault to pursue the sale with the greatest incentive. But that will produce short term results and not create the brand of honor we have as one sealed in the Name of The Lord.

No, our calling is one to perform the best service for all others. In this we are rewarded and create a long-lasting business.

Don't look out only for your own interests, but take an interest in others, too. — *Philippians 2:4*

෴

Lord Jesus, thank You for all the opportunities You have given me to serve others through providing goods and services. And thank You for all of the future opportunities I do not know of yet.

I pray that You remove any desires of greed in my business from me and replace them with generosity.

I pray that my talents, skills and knowledge will be used to help households in need and to always put others first.

All Others

⤙⤚

IT IS TEMPTING to serve prospects and individuals who provide us an obvious business incentive better than some others. Scriptural exhortation to be good to all people is wildly valuable for our Sales Ministry.

Our vision as humans can be incredibly limited. We really do not know who will be our next great opportunity for service in the future. By doing well for all people, doors open that we do not even know exist yet.

We never know, that person waiting on us at a restaurant or helping us at the service station could be our next great customer.

But always try to do good to each other and to all people. — *1 Thessalonians 5:15*

❦

Lord, You taught Samuel to see the heart of a king in David. Your will is to look to see what is inside of a person.

Father, I ask and pray that You give me Your eyes to see others and myself.

That I would never judge another person. That I would only ascribe to them what You desire for them to hear.

Bless all others I encounter today, Oh Lord.

The Greatest

SOME SALES PEOPLE are better than all others. If we cannot recognize it by observation, they will probably be glad to tell us.

It is true, the sales world is filled with huge success stories carried by even larger egos.

But we, are Sales Ministers. We are called to serve. And like Jesus, we will serve others. We do not do this to become great, but greatness is serving.

Leadership is serving. Sales is serving.

It is amazing how great prospects and clients think of us when we put them first.

The greatest among you must be a servant. — *Matthew 23:11*

✎∂

Oh, Lord I want to be the best. You have put this ambition in me. To succeed and be the best servant I can be.

But Lord, today I am humbled by Your greatness. There is nothing I can be or do that can compare.

I love, that You have put me in a call that I can serve all others.

May I be a blessing to each one today.

And that is the greatest!

Honestly

❧

MANY OF US might say, "it is best not to be poor at all..." And there is truth in this statement, because we want to provide for the needs of our clients, the results of our companies and provisions of our households.

No, the ministry of sales does not allow for poverty.

However, it is always better to be poor in spirit, than to be rich in our own ability.

The deception of trusting ourselves over God, will bring even the most skilled representative crashing down.

Better to be poor and honest than to be dishonest and rich. — *Proverbs 28:6*

❧❧

Lord, I need to be rich in You!

Anything else will not satisfy what I desire.

I know You have cattle on many hills. I know You will provide.

Thank You for all I have.

Today, I ask for more of You.

Strength in God

❧❧

ALL KINDS OF THOUGHTS come our way each day. Some of these are helpful and some are destructive.

Each day we have the choice to take thoughts and turn them into action.

In our faith, we have the power to choose life. And in our faith we have the power to encourage ourselves in the Lord.

Our persistence in our faith is crucial to move on to the next steps as a Sales Minister.

We can encourage ourselves, and find strength in God.

But David found strength in the Lord his God. — *I Samuel 30:6*

❦

As Your servant David was attacked on all sides, he encouraged himself and found strength in Your presence.

Lord, I ask for Your strength today. I know and believe in Your word.

Lord, I know and believe in Your ways.

Lord, I know and believe You have called me to this ministry today. May I follow hard after You.

A Greater Determination

❧

THERE ARE DAYS in our Sales Ministry when it seems people of all kinds present challenges against us.

We have a choice in those moments. We can agree with the voice of defeat and uncertainty.

Or we can increase our resolve in service to The Lord and our clients.

We have a tremendous call from God.

In that call, regardless of success or adversity we can "work with even greater determination"!

So I continued the work with even greater determination. — *Nehemiah 6:9*

❧❧

Lord, in You I have hope.

Lord, in You, I have confidence.

Lord, in You, I believe.

Many in my business have heard they need to be determined. That we need to be persistent to win.

Today Lord, I place all my determination in You. I know that in Your will, I can accomplish success and change lives around me.

Thank You, God for making me a vessel for this call.

ABOUT THE AUTHOR

Max J. Lambdin, (M.S. in Management), is a business executive, sales coach, author and international speaker.

He currently serves on the leadership teams of a Fortune 500 company and the Vineyard Church of Toledo.

He resides in Northwest Ohio with his wife Deborah and their three children.

www.ingramcontent.com/pod-product-compliance
Lightning Source LLC
Chambersburg PA
CBHW070813050426
42452CB00011B/2022